The Way of the Toltec Nagual

New Precepts for the Spiritual Warrior

Almine

Published by Spiritual Journeys LLC

First Edition January, 2009

Copyright 2009
MAB 998 Megatrust

By Almine
Spiritual Journeys LLC
P.O. Box 300
Newport, Oregon 97365
www.spiritualjourneys.com

Cover Illustration–Charles Frizzell
Cover Production–Pete McKeeman
Book Production—Hong-An Tran-Tien

Manufactured in the United States of America

ISBN 978-1-934070-56-7

Dedication

The release to humanity of this deeply mystical information is dedicated to the impeccable warriors who have embarked on the most profound adventure of all: the journey of self-discovery. May the innocence of your hearts and the purity of your minds bring illumination to all.

Acknowledgements

All color art has been done by Raj Singh. All pen and ink drawings have been received and drawn by Eva Pulnicki, with some contributions by Shelley Franklin. The sigils were received by Karen Folgarelli. This book has been typeset by Hong-An Tran-Tien, the cover designed by Pete McKeeman, and the cover art is by Charles Frizzell.

It is with deep gratitude that the exquisite work of these artists is acknowledged. Everyone has contributed with passion and with joy.

About the Author

Almine is endorsed and described as one of the greatest mystics of our time by world leaders and scientists alike. While other way-showers gather more and more students, she helps create more and more masters. Her work represents the cutting edge of mysticism; that place where the physical and the non-physical meet and new realities are born. It is here where change is rapid and insight comes quickly to wash away years of stagnation.

In February of 2005, Almine's body underwent a transfiguration, changing from mortal to immortal in the twinkling of an eye. Her books have been a roadmap to lead others into the same mastery and beyond. Masters populate her classes and are a fulfillment of a mission given to her in January 2005: prepare the leadership for a Golden Age about to be birthed on Earth.

Having lived as a Toltec Nagual (a specific type of mystic dedicated to a life of impeccability and setting others free from illusion) for most of her life, her insights into cosmology and man's role within the macrocosm are ground-breaking. Pushing illuminating insights even further than previous Toltecs have done, she has managed to solve mysteries that have perplexed Toltec seers for eons.

Throughout history, the majority of spiritual masters and gurus who have entered mastery have withdrawn from society. This is understandable because words seem inadequate to describe experiences such as coming face-to-face with the Infinite and the physical act of speaking becomes laborious. Almine's gift is her ability to convey these experiences by rendering the unspeakable understandable. She feels it is time for people to understand that they can choose to claim mastery as their constant reality and remain functional in society.

Words to describe the unknowable flow through her and when shared with others often leave them feeling as though they have touched the face of God. Her revelations bring answers to questions that have plagued mankind since the dawn of time, revealing the origin and meaning of human existence.

Her journey has become one of learning to live in the physical while functioning in eternal time and maintaining the delicate balance of remaining self-aware while being fully expanded.

Table of Contents

Bonus Section: The Twelve Hidden Planets

Changes in Toltec Mysticism

Introduction

In mastering the seven gates of dreaming, Toltecs have uncovered deep secrets of existence. For even as they studied the four deep stages of sleep and the three shallow ones, the microcosmic role of man taught them that life itself had been through similar stages.

Creation was conceived as part of the Infinite's dream. But as life awakened from its slumber and eventually the Infinite's dream ended, all individuated creations exited the dream. In the twinkling of an eye, all life was re-created as real. This meant that it was no longer made from the building blocks of life; it was no longer a pot made from the potter's clay. It became part of the potter; part of the one real element that contains all light, frequency, awareness, life-force, energy and power within it: holy incorruptible matter. Since October 2008 we have become part of the Infinite's Being.

In August 2006, while still in the dream, the cosmic poles reversed, shattering the moving spirals of awareness and fundamentally altering the nature of polarity. The world of the Toltec Warrior was turned upside down as many of the laws he had based his conduct on became obsolete[1]. Even something as elementary as compassion took on a whole different meaning.

1. See *The Ring of Truth*

Other than their dedication to truth, nothing has prepared the Toltecs for the even larger changes that took place as life left the Infinite's dream space and became real. We dare not look back. To do so does not serve life. All is newly created and new precepts await discovery.

There are 96 levels of teachings pertaining to the new Toltec precepts. This book reveals but one of them. There are 144 levels of information to master the DNA activations that create a potent supply of power and awareness for the Toltecs' impeccable use. Once again, we share but one of them. The ancient Toltec mystical secrets of the human body are a gateway made available to humanity at the dawn of a great renaissance of spiritual awakening.

"Kanesh viva uheres stavavi"
May the truth ring in your heart.

With dedication,
Almine

Precepts for the New Toltec Way

Flake of Purity #1

Kilestra-vesvi

There is nothing to learn and everything to know. All is available now.

Replaces: A warrior lives frugally, learning
from everything; wasting no energy.

Flake of Purity #2

Branuk-vivas-velvi

There is only one eternal fluid moment. No time exists.

Replaces: A master always compresses time by
focusing with great awareness on the details.

Flake of Purity #3

Plu-arat-nuset

A master knows that he is all things and all identities.

Replaces: A master does not admit his identity, even to himself.

Flake of Purity #4

Kraanug-uspetvi

Supported by all life, overwhelming odds cannot exist.
A master accesses all perspectives at once.

Replaces: When against overwhelming odds, we focus on the details.

Flake of Purity #5

Paaha-ulug-nasat

Trust in the interconnectedness of life and the support it
brings. Belief in self-guidance brings surrender and
the sense of being overwhelmed is eliminated.

Replaces: When against overwhelming odds,
a master surrenders to the battle.

Flake of Purity #6

Verarut-unasvi

Life seems to be the One expressing as the many. Rather, it is the many expressing as the One. In your reality, you are all that is; relationships therefore do not exist.

Replaces: We co-create all interactions in relationships.

Flake of Purity #7

Kaararat-selvavi

All mysteries are already known to the Infinite. Our quest for freedom
from the dream has been fulfilled. There is no mystery and no duty,
just the joy of living.

Replaces: We cannot solve the mysteries of existence,
but it is our duty to try.

Flake of Purity #8

Pirich-bru-aset

The only discovery is self-discovery,
which we express through our experiences.

Replaces: We are turning the unknown
into the known through our experiences.

Flake of Purity #9

Virsh-nanuvat

In each warrior's life is the knowledge that they are all that is.
Acting in a way that is life-enhancing to self benefits all.

Replaces: All solutions must benefit everyone
involved in the interaction.

Flake of Purity #10

Krechvaa-skelerug

All reveals itself through the silent surrender of our being.

Replaces: We cannot take anything at face value – nothing is as it seems.

Flake of Purity #11

Kaaresh-ustavi-kelshbahut

We dwell in incorruptible holy matter. It is the substance of all life.
All we have to do is remember it.

Replaces: We are being stalked by death.

Flake of Purity #12

Granug-viravesbi-kelestrat

Power is an irrevocably fused component of the incorruptible holy matter from which we are made. It is our inseparable birth right.

Replaces: Power tests us to determine our worthiness to wield it.

Flake of Purity #13

Pilihut-sebachtvi-urares

Humility means we stand in silence before the wonder of our being
and allow it to reveal everything to us.

Replaces: Humility means we acknowledge that we know nothing.

Flake of Purity #14

Kanabit-sebavu

There are two types of warriors; those who fluidly changed with the cosmic polarities and those who did not. The former knows that perception and power have become an inherent part of their being.

Replaces: There are two types of warriors: perception seekers and power seekers.

Flake of Purity #15

Kirtratvi-subavu

The destiny of all life-forms is to align themselves with the song of the cosmos: the Genesis of Pristine Creations.

Replaces: The destiny of all life-forms is to turn the unknown into the known through experience.

Flake of Purity #16

Branuk-vivas-velvi

Nothing is unknown to the Infinite because we dwell within its Being.
The amount we can know is limited only by our willingness to receive.

Replaces: Information can be divided into
the known, the unknown and the unknowable.

Flake of Purity #17

Paarut-minhervach

There is only one reality in existence. All octaves have been reduced to a single note, the incorruptible holy matter of the Infinite's Being.

Replaces: There are 32 other realities man can assemble or visit.

Flake of Purity #18

Pilisatvi-uresba

The luminous cocoon has collapsed into the physical, mirroring the cosmic implosion that took place during the past decade.
Complexity is yielding to simplicity.

Replaces: The luminous cocoon surrounds the human body.

Flake of Purity #19

Salvevi-unasvi

The assemblage point has become a field superimposed over the body of
man. All realities can be accessed within our being.

Replaces: The assemblage point lies as a bright ball
on the edge of the luminous cocoon of man.

Flake of Purity #20

Kaarchba-nunasat

All realities have merged into one, as have mind and feeling. It requires
allowing ourselves to see and dissolve old obsolete boundaries.

Replaces: It requires silencing the dialogue of the mind
to maintain a shift in realities.

Flake of Purity #21

Paaletvi-hurasvi

Inner dialogue within a master who has moved beyond the place of the silent mind is a choice. When all perspectives are engaged at once, the dialogue of the surface mind cannot convince us that it is all there is.

Replaces: Inner dialogue traps us in identity.

Flake of Purity #22

Elash-ani-heresva

Linear time and linear becoming have ceased to exist. We are free to effect the fluid unfolding of the moment through the purity of our intent.

Replaces: We have a designated destiny (multiple lifetimes) and fate (this specific lifetime).

Flake of Purity #23

Bru-at-suvavi

The Toltec's challenge is to live the fluidity for which his training has prepared him and embrace the new reality of growth through grace.

Replaces: The Toltec Naguals' goal is to lead others
to freedom from illusion.

Flake of Purity #24

Paalish-minurak

There is only the now – the place where all truth is accessible. Through
the interconnectedness of life what is known by one is available to all.

Replaces: We need to recapitulate (gain the insights of) the past
to enable us to see behind the appearances.

Flake of Purity #25

Ku-uvaves-hereshvi

Personal labels can be assumed to aid in manifesting intent.
They only obscure truth when we believe them to be all that we are.

Replaces: We cannot have clear feelings (non-cognitive information)
if we have personal labels.

Flake of Purity #26

Kelsat-minavesbi

When we are all beings, there is only One Life. Relationship cannot have an actual existence. It is a role we play within ourselves.

Replaces: Relationship is the temple for spiritual growth.

Flake of Purity #27

Kalesh-privak-minuset

The warrior is always ready to embrace the truth of the moment and to change directions in order to follow the adventure of self-discovery.

Replaces: A warrior is always ready to make his last stand here and now.

Flake of Purity #28

Purs-manivik-suvetvi

All realities have merged into one and the six lightbodies of man, including the 7th, have collapsed into a unified field within the physical.

Replaces: The 7th lightbody of man contains lightfibers that give access to other realities.

Flake of Purity #29

Elavamik-nanuvash

Mind and emotion have been irrevocably bonded in healing duality.
Combined they form awareness. Mind domination is now
a choice and enlightenment can come in a moment.

Replaces: The alternative to battling for freedom
is slavery to social conditioning.

Flake of Purity #30

Vaarch-sasena-hetvi

A master can temporarily assume a world view
in order to effectively manifest it.

Replaces: A master has no world view.

Flake of Purity #31

Paalavik-herechva

Growth is exponential and immediate. Because of the
interconnectedness of life when one grows,
all grow in fluid transfiguration.

Replaces: Transformation, transmutation and transfiguration
are the three stages of growth.

Flake of Purity #32

Nunas-setvavi

We dwell within the Infinite's Being where all potential is immediately
available to the extent we are willing to receive it.
The necessity to grow is a fallacy.

Replaces: We lose ground when we rest on our laurels.
Toltecs call this 'succumbing to old age'.

Flake of Purity #33

Kananesh-sebatvi

We entered spaceless space as a cosmos in October 2007.
All directions have folded into one, as did the building blocks of life.

Replaces: The seven directions are represented throughout all life-forms.

Flake of Purity #34

Araras-kilhaspavi

In living authentically from the heart we come home to ourselves.
All is available to us now in embracing the fullness of the moment.

Replaces: There is no point of arrival.

Flake of Purity #35

Brunash-skelavi

Linear growth is obsolete. Exponential growth comes in an instant through the flowering of the heart. Growth no longer comes through overcomings, but by embracing wholeness.

Replaces: There are stages of spiritual mastery with testings.

Flake of Purity #36

Kirit-harasparanut

Death has no place in the fabric of existence: the incorruptible holy matter of the Infinite's Being. The master savors
the one fluid moment that never ends.

Replaces: Death is an advisor, enabling us to live
from heightened awareness at all times.

Flake of Purity #37

Baranut-skelhavasbi

Living from the heart without the need to understand where it leads requires a familiarity with the gentle voice of its promptings.

Replaces: We stalk our self to determine our motives at all times.

Flake of Purity #38

Klubach-setvavi

Living within the Infinite's Being is to live in the fullness of an inexhaustible supply. Acknowledging the never-ending Source of abundance increases its accessibility.

Replaces: To take more than we need is to deplete ourselves and our environment.

Flake of Purity #39

Kaleshnar-suvetvi

Living from the heart produces the unpredictable
spontaneity mind would deny us.

Replaces: To act predictably is to fall prey
to being tracked by adversaries.

Flake of Purity #40

Piritnurstavi-uvechspi

Acknowledging that the unreal cannot impact the real,
we surrender to the perfection of life.

Replaces: There are three types of resistance: that which reflects,
that which conducts and that which absorbs.

Flake of Purity #41

Kurusatvi-nanuvach

Power and perception are both threads in the tapestry of the One Life.
Both are elements of incorruptible holy matter of which all life consists.
We need not chase either – all exists within our being.

Replaces: We stalk power by seeking perception.
Power is a side-effect of perception.

Flake of Purity #42

Blublat-irvanut

All self-perception is a lens into the Infinite's perception.

Replaces: All perception is self-perception.

Flake of Purity #43

Paalinsk-haravit-nesba

Energy is fused with incorruptible holy matter from which we are made.
How much consciousness we possess is determined
by how much we surrender to life.

Replaces: Energy's availability determines levels of consciousness.

Flake of Purity #44

Vrubisk-ululat

A master with authenticity embraces life.

Replaces: A master is a warrior against illusion.

Flake of Purity #45

Ku-uhur-natvi

All etheric bodies have merged with the physical. The destinies of man no longer exist. We create pristinely from the heart in the moment.

Replaces: Our higher self designs our life and then we resist it.
This is known as 'the madness within the dream'.

Flake of Purity #46

Kaarch-bravis-plura

Mind-at-rest has ceased to exist as presence and life-force
and awareness have merged back into incorruptible matter.

Replaces: Consciousness consists of mind at rest;
having presence and life force, but no awareness.

Flake of Purity #47

Nushba-erekvi-narspa

The unknown can be instantly accessed through the
silence within. All realities have merged into one.
The assemblage point has become a field.

Replaces: We use the art of dreaming to access the unknown,
an expanded state accomplished by small
shifts of the assemblage point.

Flake of Purity #48

Puhurspave-nunashvi

The honor of a warrior is his innocence of heart and purity of mind, coupled with the confidence that in full awareness in the moment, he may know all things.

Replaces: The shield of a warrior is his humility in knowing he knows nothing, coupled with confidence in being fully aware.

Flake of Purity #49

Klaarsbaruh-ninesva

The force behind the unfolding of the cosmos is the Infinite's Intent;
something man can experience by aligning with it.

Replaces: The force behind the unfolding of the cosmos is the Infinite's
Intent; something man cannot comprehend.

Flake of Purity #50

Truma-hubach-savi

All the cosmos stands revealed through self-knowledge. All knowledge reveals itself through effortless knowing within the silence.

Replaces: Most of the cosmos is incomprehensible from man's limited vantage point.

Flake of Purity #51

Laminihur-salasbi

There is neither past nor future and progression is no longer cyclical.
Awareness no longer moves in spirals, but responds
to love, praise and gratitude.

Replaces: Life's insights repeat themselves in
cycles of 7, 12 or 20 years.

Flake of Purity #52

Virsti-uvabach

The shattering of the spirals of awareness during the cosmic pole
reversal in August 2006 stopped their linear movement
across space. The nature of light has become telepathic
and it travels exponentially. Time no longer exists.

Replaces: Time is the movement of anything,
such as awareness or light across space.

Flake of Purity #53

Plu-ararak-netvi

In October 2007, as the directions folded into the direction of within, we entered spaceless space. All bands of compassion became one: Unconditional Oneness.

Replaces: Vast frequency bands exist that all Creation consists of. They constitute the directions and determine their nature.

Flake of Purity #54

Ustatvi-heresbak

As the microcosm, man mirrors the macrocosmic unifying of the bands
of compassion. The seven bodies of man, comprising the
luminous cocoon, have collapsed into the physical.
All resources are readily available.

Replaces: Naguals have double luminous cocoons which
enables them to have more energy and other resources.

Flake of Purity #55

Kra-a-ganuk-spavi

Power has become irrevocably fused with incorruptible holy matter.
Change no longer uses transformation, transmutation and
transfiguration, but occurs through
transfigurative regeneration.

Replaces: Power is released when one pattern or template of existence
yields to a higher one. Patterns transfigure because of
increased perception.

Flake of Purity #56

Paha-unusva-hereshbi

With the removal of all pre-destined templates of life, such as
the matrix, grids and other programs, there is no preset
destiny nor are there key moments that are part of a
predetermined plan. Life is gloriously produced
in the moment through authentic living.

Replaces: Toltecs await with awareness key moments
that bring opportunities for positive change.

Flake of Purity #57

Kilstatvi-heruhik

Change became exponential when the spirals of awareness shattered during the cosmic pole reversal. The key to embracing such change is to shed obsolete belief systems and expectations.

Replaces: For change to be effective, it has to be decisive and large, implemented one step at a time.

Flake of Purity #58

Kru-uhanushbapra

There is no limit to what can be known when
the mind is pure and the heart is innocent.

Replaces: We cannot know what lies outside of cosmic life,
it is therefore the unknowable.

Flake of Purity #59

Velskla-ninuvit

All energy and resources are available within holy incorruptible matter
from which we are made. Polarity has become a unified
field – polarity has been healed.

Replaces: All life pulses between positive and negative poles – this
provides the energy for life in the cosmos.

Flake of Purity #60

Kirichba-uvravit

The entire cosmos is made from the Infinite's holy incorruptible matter.
There is no opposite matter. Energy, light and frequency have become
inseparably bonded to matter.

Replaces: Opposite light and frequency attract;
opposite matter and energy repel.

Flake of Purity #61

Ululu-sklavaa

With opposite poles no longer pulsing, equilibrium is the nature of reality. From the soil of equilibrium, flowering occurs.

Replaces: Perfect equilibrium causes stasis, and stasis causes death.

Flake of Purity #62

Aranaspahur-esklavi

The contraction of vision that focused on the details and produced duality has been changed. Humanity is able to see all perspectives at once.

Replaces: Duality is the result of the peculiarity of vision and focus of man.

Flake of Purity #63

Ruchpa-sklererot

There is only one choice in the cosmos: what is life-enhancing
and what is more life-enhancing.

Replaces: There is only one choice in the cosmos:
what is life-enhancing and what is not.

Flake of Purity #64

Alasvaa-hurnastavi

We exited the dream of the Infinite in October 2008. Life has become real, being now formed from the Infinite's incorruptible matter.

Replaces: Physical life with its forgetfulness of our larger self and its misperceptions is regarded as the dream.

Flake of Purity #65

Aratklavavi

Death as the tumbling force of the movement of the spirals of awareness
has ceased to exist since the shattering of the spirals in August 2006.
Having been re-created from the Infinite's Being, rather than the
building blocks of existence, life has become immortal.

Replaces: In living impeccably and in full surrender to life,
we earn the right to overcome death.

Flake of Purity #66

Vurs-stetparanuch

Opposition is no longer the way of growth, nor is growth required. Hardships are no longer needed as we move into a deathless society.

Replaces: Death is a tumbling force, pummeling man; hardships are its allies.

Flake of Purity #67

Kavarich-ereleshustra

Inherent flaws consisted of unyielded potential that blocked light.
All life has been re-created with all potential available.

Replaces: Our strong suits lie in the overcoming of our inherent flaws.

Flake of Purity #68

Kaalsbapratnut

In the clarity of the availability of our full potential, there is no longer a
duty to learn. Illusion as a teacher is obsolete.

Replaces: It is our duty to learn from our brother's folly
so that his experiences can yield their fruits.

Flake of Purity #69

Arlasklatminur

The true reality of the cosmos no longer includes either mirrors or
prisms that refract light. We are no longer required to learn
from environmental mirrors.

Replaces: Our environment is the mirror of what we are or what we
judge, what we've lost or have yet to develop.

Flake of Purity #70

Urch-vruvavesbi

We have become that which contains all knowledge – it reveals itself by staying in the moment within silence of the mind.

Replaces: Practicing fluidity enables dreaming – an expanded viewpoint that reveals reality non-cognitively.

Flake of Purity #71

Aalsat-birtlhut

Addiction occurs when the self is abandoned. There is nothing
that constitutes testing. Linear growth has been
replaced by exponential flowering.

Replaces: Addiction is part of the testing in
the stages of spiritual growth.

Flake of Purity #72

Kalasbi-vurach

Rage, fear, pain and protectiveness became unreal frequencies as the cosmos ascended and the four basic pairs of emotions were replaced by the twelve pure pairs of emotions.

Replaces: Rage is the result of suppressed light and is used to break up that which is stuck.

Flake of Purity #73

Minhur-ustatvi-kalbash

When created life was used as a mirror for the Infinite, portions were
not understood because mirrors reflect backwards. We have left the
stages of the dream, where life has been a reflection, and
solved all mysteries of beingness.

Replaces: The part of the cosmos most reluctant to yield to a higher
order is what we call darkness – the portions of the
Infinite's Being as yet unknown.

Flake of Purity #74

Paarehut-unas

We do not need to engage the unreal. It has no value within the true
Being of the Infinite now that the unknown portions of existence
have been solved.

Replaces: Anything to which we deny the right to exist is strengthened,
either within us or within our environment.

Flake of Purity #75

Vlubas-arat-venasvi

There is no past. There are no longer surrounding fields – they have
collapsed within. There is no longer a set of specific insights
we have to get – just the joyous discovery of life.

Replaces: Unyielded insights create constrictions in the surrounding
fields of the body, causing karma.

Flake of Purity #76

Minihur-kurat

The cosmos no longer moves in giant arcs as its propelling force – the spirals of moving awareness – no longer exist.

Replaces: The cosmos folds in and out, like a giant tube torus, creating the in-breath and out-breath of the Infinite.

Flake of Purity #77

Aarshva-velavi

Life is no longer challenging us to grow, but waiting for us to explore.

Replaces: By embracing our challenges as our greatest teachers, we can turn darkness to light, one step at a time.

Flake of Purity #78

Pitrihur-selvavi

The consciousness of an individual is determined by how much of life's
resources his attitudes permit him to access. All light is contained
in the holy incorruptible matter we are made of.

Replaces: When we refer to an individual's consciousness, we refer to
how much light an individual can contain.

Flake of Purity #79

Trinibas-urasvi

The burden of being the pivot point for the growth of the cosmos has been removed from the few and re-distributed to the many. Wherever authentic living takes place, life flourishes.

Replaces: The wayshowers on Earth are the warriors who have come to do battle against illusion, armed with innocence and impeccability.

Flake of Purity #80

Trunis-ulubas

There is only one tone in the cosmos containing all others. Emotion and perception can no longer function separately. As part of healing duality, they have been bonded together.

Replaces: There are twelve pure pairs of emotions in the cosmos.

Flake of Purity #81

Kaarstat-ulesbi

The meaning of life is the same for all beings: Adoration in Action.

Replaces: We cannot hope to understand the meaning of life, thus we seek only the clarity to know our next step.

Flake of Purity #82

Nunmer-salvavi

When energy is bonded with holy incorruptible matter it cannot be lost.
But it can more fully be accessed by living with
an open heart in the moment.

Replaces: In order to avoid being taken by surprise, the warrior, when
confronted by the unknown, believes without believing (acting as
though he understands). Surprise and shock drain energy
and lower consciousness.

Flake of Purity #83

Isalmanur-etravi

All light bodies or higher aspects of ourselves have been consolidated into the physical. Our guidance comes directly from the Infinite's Intent.

Replaces: Toltecs strive to cooperate with life as designed by our higher selves. This is called the 'intelligent cooperation with life'.

Flake of Purity #84

Estabil-etretvi

As duality was healed, life became androgynous and genderless.

Replaces: All life is divided into feminine (receptive) and masculine (pro-active) components.

Flake of Purity #85

Kisilnanuvit

The symbols of our dreams point out where life can be lived more
authentically and with more joyous discovery.

Replaces: The symbols of our dreams tell us what we have
overlooked in the lessons of our day.

Flake of Purity #86

Ustaanumir-velabit

Disease only existed as a reality when illusion existed within the
cosmos. We no longer receive promptings from our higher
aspects, since they have ceased to exist. We may live from
our expanded self as long as we do not disengage
from life. We may live from our contracted self
as long as we remember we are much more.

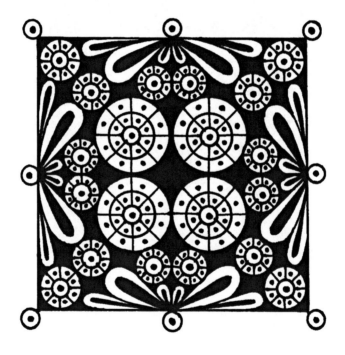

Replaces: Disease is the prompting from our higher selves to indicate
where we are not living from our largest self.

Flake of Purity #87

Aalech-haaras-traumir

Life yields all secrets to a receptive heart in the quietness of the mind.

Replaces: Any battle the warrior engages in has to have a worthy stake:
unyielded perception.

Flake of Purity #88

Ustabal-karanech

The fusing of emotion and perception has produced attitudes. Attitudes of enlightenment arise when we are aligned with the Infinite's Intent – the state of Unconditional Oneness.

Replaces: Perception yields emotion and emotion yields perception.

Flake of Purity #89

Vurasparut-unasvi

Thoughts alone disturb innocence since innocence is only found in the
moment. Thought and emotions have been joined into one.
Thoughts are now a life-enhancing option.

Replaces: Thoughts arise as a resistance to life
and pull us out of the moment.

Flake of Purity #90

Kasalnit-mitrur-aravat

Mindlessness and thought, bonded to emotion, are both life-enhancing
options - as long as we remember we are not our experiences.
We must remember too the value of our experiences.

Replaces: Cultivating mindlessness is the goal of mastery.

Flake of Purity #91

Pu-achna-salvavi

When the One expresses as the many through Its creations,
it is for the purpose of being delighted.

Replaces: When the One expresses as the many through Its creations,
it is for the purpose of learning about the mysteries of Its Being.

Flake of Purity #92

Hurstanamir-estava

All frequency bands have blended into one: Unconditional Oneness.
Directions are obsolete. We are aligned to the one band of existence,
for in it we dwell and have our being.

Replaces: All things in the cosmos are by their nature aligned to one
direction or another. The directions are the result of
multiple frequency bands.

Flake of Purity #93

Ka-urut-unasbi

All subpersonalities have blended into one, existing together and expressing together at all times. Their roles have been implemented and understood by the Infinite.

Replaces: The subpersonalities are the destiny of man to live and understand.

Flake of Purity #94

Estava-vinabir

All pre-ordained destinies were fulfilled when illusion was solved. All fate ceased when we exited from the dream. We are free to write the scripts of our lives.

Replaces: Destiny is the purpose of all the other lives, our individuation has lived. Fate pertains to this life's mission.

Flake of Purity #95

Ku-uhalas-piret

The disciplined warrior does not treat the past as real by looking back.
Time has ceased to exist. The moment reveals itself in silence.

Replaces: Silence of the mind is achieved through disciplined
perseverance in extracting from past experience unyielded insight.

Flake of Purity #96

Paarich-nunstat

It is in alignment with the moment that the Infinite Intent can
flow through us. Aligned with Infinite Intent, we live
in the most life-enhancing way possible.

Replaces: We prepare for the worst in order to be able to expect the best.

Flake of Purity #97

Arlabit-bistruvar

The warrior's purpose is to vigilantly guard the authenticity of his life, guarding against all external and internal programming.

Replaces: The warrior's battle is to extract perception through experience.

Flake of Purity #98

Ku-uharut-valsat

There are no outer and inner realities. The cosmos lives in spaceless space. That is why there is no relationship.

Replaces: The master changes the outer world by changing within. The outer is but an inner reflection.

Flake of Purity #99

Bitret-aralasklava

Life as a reflection is an obsolete concept. All forms of life,
even inanimate objects, are made from the Infinite's Being
and therefore alive and real. All lives within us.

Replaces: The only real part of anyone's existence is himself. All else is
but a reflection of his inner reality and cannot be experienced directly.

Flake of Purity #100

Estech-haralesvi

All parallel existences have either merged because they were life-enhancing enough to be assimilated, or they have been dissolved.

Replaces: There are 32 additional realities man can access
that are available as parallel existences.

Flake of Purity #101

Kilibrut-hunesbi

All notes of existence have folded into one. Realms are hidden only
because their kingdoms choose to hide from man.

Replaces: Higher octaves of existence have folded into higher notes of
existence. The hidden realms are now much more accessible.

Flake of Purity #102

Stelasplava-kranunes

Because the internal and external realities have merged, there are nine
rings of incorruptible white magic[2] available to man.

Replaces: There are two types of magic: first ring magic that uses
external techniques and second ring magic that uses internal techniques.

2. For more information about the nine rings of incorruptible white magic,
see www.ancientshamanism.com

Flake of Purity #103

Vurut-kabis-unet-trava

All nine rings have limits. Affecting life by living in
unconditional oneness has none.

Replaces: First ring magic is limited. Second ring magic is limitless.

Flake of Purity #104

Kiritnatvi-heluhit

When entering the God-kingdom, the Nagual cracks his cocoon into
additional splits, creating a total of seven prongs. The further
evolution of one who has left the human kingdom cracks it
yet again into a total of 20 prongs. The luminous
cocoon is now inside the body.

Replaces: A Nagual cracks his luminous cocoon into three or four
prongs, depending on the type of information he or she works with.

Flake of Purity #105

Isitrananur-hetvi

Higher life uses a different sequence: 1, 3, 7, 12, 20, 33, 54, 72, 96, 144.
Light traveling linearly is obsolete. Geometry as a reality is no more.
Light, bonded with frequency, exists as a field.

Replaces: Life is created through sacred dynamic geometry and
according to the Fibonacci sequence.

Flake of Purity #106

Piranur-skanuvach

Life is no longer a process of seeking to become.
It is instead a flowering of where we are.

Replaces: Life is a never-ending journey of gathering perception.

Flake of Purity #107

Vurat-piruhar

Life and its creations are the many expressing as the One.

Replaces: Life and its creations are the One expressing as the many.

Flake of Purity #108

Kalabu-suvatru

The separation of white light was the beginning of duality and the
unreal. Duality has been healed. The reality of separately
existing colors has been removed.

Replaces: All life expresses according to the primary trinity of red
(pro-active), blue (receptive) and yellow (neutral). Represented by
the attitudes of love, praise and gratitude.

The Forming of Colors

"In the beginning white light I had
Formless and eternal I contemplated My Being
In innocence I tried the unthinkable: something new and unknown
Never before did the unknown exist

I separated portions within, to examine them
Duality arose and My light shone through the prism of separation
A rainbow was created that lay around me like a rose
It created a boundary within My Being; that which is without boundaries

I conceived the possibility that creation can be made through separation
My thinking shattered My innocence
Further petals formed of the rose
I thought I was enclosed by it

I know, as experiential knowledge grew,
That separation is illusion and cannot create wholeness,
That beauty cannot exist where unrealness is
My fascination with refracted light served not life

I overvalued the contribution that separation made
In suggesting the creation of individuated life
In the oneness of My Being life would've arose
Individuated and pure, pristine and whole

No need for hardship opposition and death
But because they were, appreciation of life is also"

Additional information about how life formed was only released to
humankind when the library of the secrets of the angels opened on
Mount Seboheth in the middle of January 2009. At that time, Almine
was able to translate the huge gold tablets to receive the additional
information[3].

3. See *The Gift of Angels: The Restoration of Angelic Powers to Humanity*

The Toltec Gateways of
Power in the Human Body

The Toltec Gateways of the Thirteen Primary Joints

The human body as a magical instrument for accessing various perspectives of reality and revealing the perfection of pristine creation is the source of the two outer (the 8th and 9th) rings of magic (see also www.wayofthetoltecnagual.com)

The 8th ring utilizes the 13 main joints of the body in order to gain eternal perspectives. Discomfort in any joint area indicates that the perspective associated with that joint is too limited, rigid or is an obsolete part of the dream.

The joints are also connected to the 12 hidden planets around the Earth as well as the Earth itself. These planets exert influence during specific hours of the day[4]. There are therefore advantageous times to clear specific joints associated with them.

The method of clearing joints of all obsolete remnants of the dream in which separation was thought to exist, enables us to become one with eternal perspectives. This in turn greatly enhances the personal power available to us.

Firstly, the misperception from past debris is identified and self-work is done to correct it.

The symbol for the gate of the joint is placed on the joint to open the mystical gate located there.

Then, call the name of the angel corresponding to the joint and sign its sigil in the air over the joint[5].

The Portal to Infinite Presence is held above the joint with the left hand.

Through the Portal in your left hand, send the 13 Wheels of

4. See *Opening the Doors of Heaven* for the Zhong-Galabruk clock and www.astrology-of-isis.com
5. See page 181

Purification by holding them in your right hand (Number 1 is at the bottom and Number 13 is at the top) above the Portal to Infinite Presence. With intent, send them through the portal into the gate of the joint.

Put the 13 Wheels of Purification down. Pick up the stack of 13 Wheels of Fullness with your right hand (Number 13 is again on top), holding them above the portal in your left hand.

With intent, send the 13 Wheels of Fullness through the Portal into the gate of the joint.

How to Activate DNA Codes for Higher Life to Be Manifested

To manifest a more perfect environment in our lives, that more closely reveals the Infinite's creation rather than the sub-creation of man, DNA codes are activated. These previous tools, plus the addition of the four sacred wheels of DNA activation are used.

Steps to DNA Activation:

Using the previous method, do all 13 joints in order, starting with the left ankle.

As each joint is completed as previously described, put the additional four wheels into that joint as well – the Wheels of DNA activation.

Put the Wheels of Fullness down. Pick up the four wheels of DNA activation in your right hand, hold it over the portal in your left hand (Wheel 4 is on top).

Send the four wheels through the Portal into the joint gate. Do this with each joint as the previously given clearings are completed.

Understanding the Thirteen Joints

Toltec seers have always recognized the archetypal nature of man and the Earth. The 13 joints of man correspond to the 13 tectonic plates of the Earth. Indigenous people called the Earth 'Turtle Island'. They under stood that, like the turtle shell, the Earth had thirteen segments. The cosmos itself mirrored this prior to its ascension in 2005. Thereafter, it became more complex as depicted in the image of the Rose.

The Thirteen Joints

1) Left Ankle: Mistakes you think you made. All who have survived the purging of non-life enhancing beings during the ascension are victorious beings. Our accomplishments throughout eons of existence are therefore far outweighing seeming mistakes.

2) Right Ankle: Regrets over risks we shouldn't or should've taken. As life has woken up from the dream, the tyranny of left-brain is released. Left-brain demanded surety before acting.

3) Left knee: What others did to you is stored here. The past dream didn't really happen. All that have earned the right to live are newly created. It would be as illogical to blame someone for dreaming of them.

4) Right knee: What you did to others can be painful unless we realize that it too was a dream and that we didn't have the same perception and emotional clarity then. In addition, no one is a victim and all are co-creators in an interaction.

5) Left hip: Being wrongly judged. In the dream the majority of beings were not made by the Infinite Mother, but were artificial intelligences made by imposter gods and goddesses, designed to produce opposition for light-workers.

6) Right hip: Body issues. Wishing we were taller, fatter, thinner. Humanity is the root race for the cosmos. As such the bodily diversity is needed. Each one is beautiful just as they are.

7) Left wrist: What you lost can haunt one, but only if the self-belief is lacking that we can accomplish not only as much, but so much more because we are clearer and life is ascending.

8) Right wrist: What we didn't accomplish is usually measured against outside circumstances when true accomplishment lies within and can't be measured.

9) Left elbow: Issues related to aging. We are metamorphosing into super-human immortality. To bring about a new paradigm, we must live it. Someone younger is just as suitable as someone older for our partner or our boss or to fulfill responsibility.

10) Right elbow: Possessions we wanted or lost. We have carefully designed life to maximize growth and experiential learning. It is inconceivable to suppose that a life of affluence is a preferable one; or to measure success by it.

11) Left shoulder: Opportunities lost. We make our opportunities, no one else does. It is not a haphazard occurrence and therefore we can make the same and more opportunities again.

12) Right shoulder: What we should've known; hindsight makes things quite clear and so does additional growth arising from our mistake. This makes it seem possible to have known it before. Yet insights build upon each other like bricks build a wall.

13) Neck joint: Being abandoned and alone. The greatest illusion is that of our separateness; of thinking that we stand alone when every action of every being affects all life. The inter-connectedness of life, sustains and supports us in every conceivable way.

Left Ankle

Gate of Purity of the Heart

Right Ankle

Gate of Loving Learning

Left Knee

Gate of Harmony in Nature

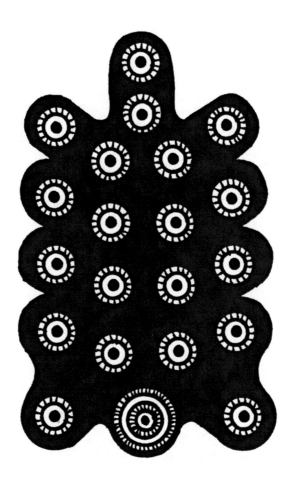

Right Knee

Gate of Harmony in Etheric Worlds

Left Hip

Gate of Joyful Reunion

Right Hip

Gate of Recharging of All Life

Left Wrist

Gate of Awakening to Fullness of Life

Right Wrist

Gate of Healing Within

Left Elbow

Gate of Graceful Shift Beyond Horizon

Right Elbow

Gate of Releasing Memories of the Past

Left Shoulder

Gate of Closing the Past

Right Shoulder

Gate of New Beginnings

Neck Joint

Gate of No Gate

The Portal to Infinite Presence

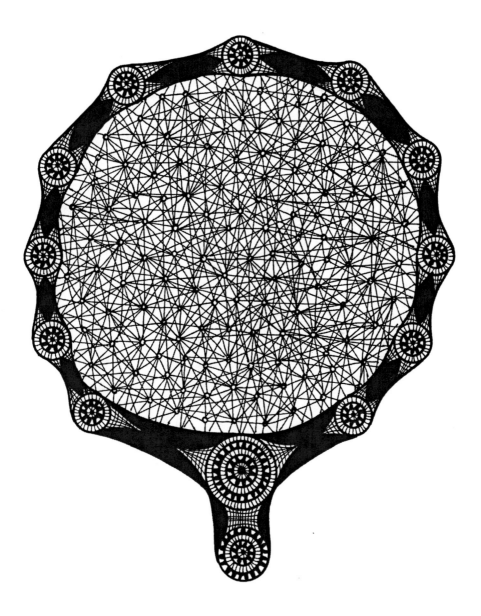

Wheel of Purification Number I

Wheel of Purification of Mistakes You Think You Made

Wheel of Purification Number 2

Wheel of Purification of Regrets Over Risks Taken or Not Taken

Wheel of Purification Number 3

Wheel of Purification of What Others Did to You

Wheel of Purification Number 4

Wheel of Purification of What You Did to Others

Wheel of Purification Number 5

Wheel of Purification of Being Judged by Others Unfairly

Wheel of Purification Number 6

Wheel of Purification of Judgement of the Body and Body
Issues due to Terror Felt in Our Vast Beingness

Wheel of Purification Number 7

Wheel of Purification of What You Feel You Have Lost

Wheel of Purification Number 8

Wheel of Purification of What You Did Not Accomplish

Wheel of Purification Number 9

Wheel of Purification of Aging Through Linear Time

Wheel of Purification Number 10

Wheel of Purification of Possessions You Wanted or Lost

Wheel of Purification Number II

Wheel of Purification of Opportunities Lost

Wheel of Purification Number 12

Wheel of Purification of What You Should Have Known

Wheel of Purification Number 13

Wheel of Purification of Being Abandoned or Alone

Wheel of Fullness Number I

Wheel of Recognition of the Infallibility of the Unfolding Life

Wheel of Fullness Number 2

Wheel of Recognition of the Everchanging Potential Available in the Moment

Wheel of Fullness Number 3

Wheel of Recognition of Individual Sovereignty

Wheel of Fullness Number 4

Wheel of Recognition of the Innocence of All Actions

Wheel of Fullness Number 5

Wheel of Recognition of the Infinite Worth of Each Life Form

Wheel of Fullness Number 6

Wheel of Recognition of the Perfection of All Life

Wheel of Fullness Number 7

Wheel of Recognition That There is Only Increase

Wheel of Fullness Number 8

Wheel of Recognition of Victorious Life

Wheel of Fullness Number 9

Wheel of Recognition of the Fluid Eternal Moment

Wheel of Fullness Number 10

Wheel of Recognition That is the One Life

Wheel of Fullness Number II

Wheel of Recognition that Life Responds to Our Intent

Wheel of Fullness Number 12

Wheel of Recognition of Accessibility of All Knowledge Through Surrender

Wheel of Fullness Number 13

Wheel of Unconditional Oneness

The First Wheel of DNA Activation

Combined DNA Field of 12x12 Clusters of DNA Strands

The Second Wheel of DNA Activation

Wheel of the Opening of the Centre of DNA
A Portal to Higher Creations

The Third Wheel of DNA Activation

Wheel of the Restoration of the Oneness of White Light

The Fourth Wheel of DNA Activation

Wheel of Ecstatic Birthing Into Union With Infinite Being

Sigils for the

New Toltec Precepts

Symbols vs. Sigils (Excerpt from Life of Miracles)

To understand sigils, we must first understand what symbols entail. We will also need to know the meanings of sigils in order to properly understand and utilize them as they are given later in this book.

A symbol **represents** something, whereas a sigil **describes** something. When someone sees a BMW or a Mercedes symbol, it represents upper middle-class vehicles of quality and distinction. On the other hand, the symbol for a Rolls Royce or Bentley represents elite vehicles that speak of a privileged lifestyle of dignity and wealth.

So much is deduced just from one symbol. A Rolls Royce evokes images of walled estates, chauffeurs, enough and accustomed money as opposed to the symbol of a Ferrari which speaks of more flamboyant taste.

Whereas symbols are common in our everyday world, the use of sigils is virtually forgotten. Even in mystery schools, their hidden knowledge eludes most mystics. But throughout the cosmos all beings of expanded awareness utilize sigils and only a few left-brain-oriented races use symbols and those primarily in alphabets. The reason is this:

If we use the word 'LOVE', we have combined four symbols (letters representing certain sounds) to make one symbol (the word that represents a feeling). But love is one of the building blocks of the cosmos, like space or energy. It can also represent many different nuances within the emotion of love (which is the desire to include) and many other disfunctionality and degrees of need we mistakenly call 'love.'

As we can see, the symbol or word can be very misleading since what it represents to one may not be what it represents to another. The sigil for love describes the quality or frequency of what is meant. It maps out the exact frequency of the emotion.

The sigil for someone's name would do the same. As the person or being rises in frequency, the sigil will change to reflect that. In the case of angels, even their names change. That is why the angel names or the goddess names have changed as the cosmos and Earth have ascended to a much higher frequency[6]. In these higher realms the languages are different and reflect the higher frequencies.

When a person has accomplished a major task within the cosmos pertaining to the agreement they made with the Infinite, they also receive a 'meaning' with its accompanying sigil. When a being is called to do a task meant for the highest good, that being will come if you have its name and meaning. The being absolutely must come if, in addition, you have the sigil for the name and meaning.

Having someone's sigil is like having that person's phone number. Sigils not only describe what they represent, but are a means to communicate with what they represent.

---

6. See higher goddess names in *Secrets of the Hidden Realms*

108 Sigils for the Flakes of Purity

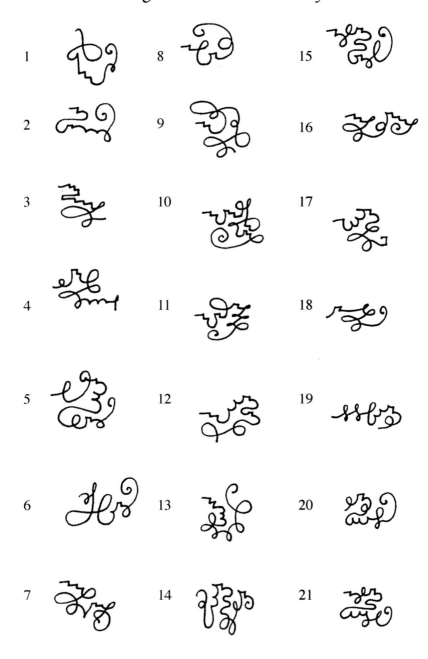

108 Sigils for the Flakes of Purity (continued)

22   29   36

23   30   37

24   31   38

25   32   39

26   33   40

27   34   41

28   35   42

108 Sigils for the Flakes of Purity (continued)

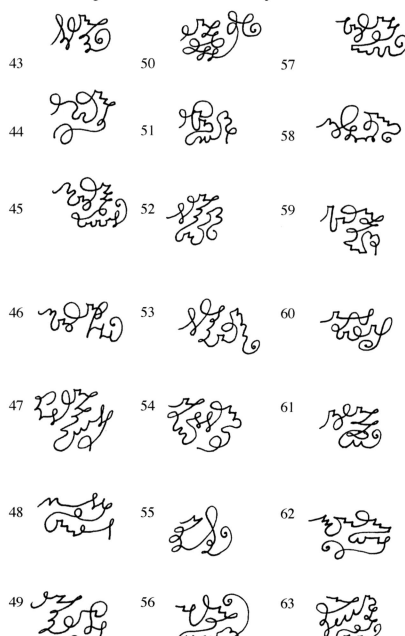

43

44

45

46

47

48

49

50

51

52

53

54

55

56

57

58

59

60

61

62

63

108 Sigils for the Flakes of Purity (continued)

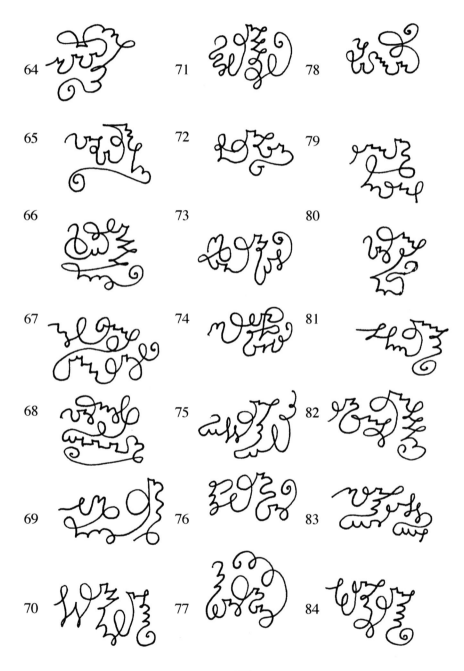

108 Sigils for the Flakes of Purity (continued)

85

92

99

86

93

100

87

94

101

88

95

102

89

96

103

90

97

104

91

98

105

108 Sigils for the Flakes of Purity (continued)

106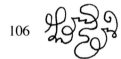

107

108

Angel Sigils for the Thirteen Joints

1. Left Ankle
   Leketinu

2. Right Ankle
   Blimiku

3. Left Knee
   Sakakalu

4. Right Knee
   Ririkna

5. Left Hip
   Siheklavesh

6. Right Hip
   Bibisibi

7. Left Wrist
   Rirelvik

8. Right Wrist
   Blihini

9. Left Elbow
   Renimu

10. Right Elbow
    Reniuma

11. Left Shoulder
    Kikesh

12. Right Shoulder
    Lavekmini

13. Neck
    Hini-hema
    -vukuma

The Lords of Light Who
Guard the Toltec Precepts

Guardian Lords of Light

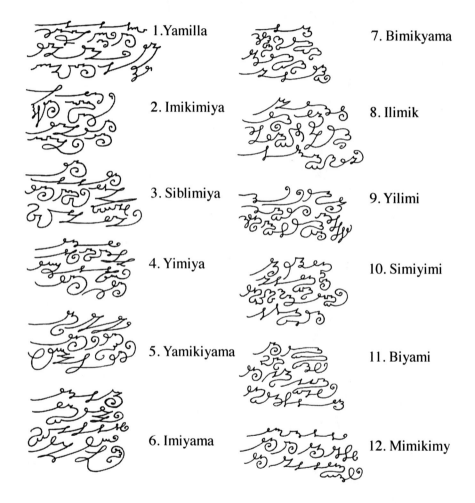

1. Yamilla
2. Imikimiya
3. Siblimiya
4. Yimiya
5. Yamikiyama
6. Imiyama
7. Bimikyama
8. Ilimik
9. Yilimi
10. Simiyimi
11. Biyami
12. Mimikimy

Guardian Lords of Light (continued)

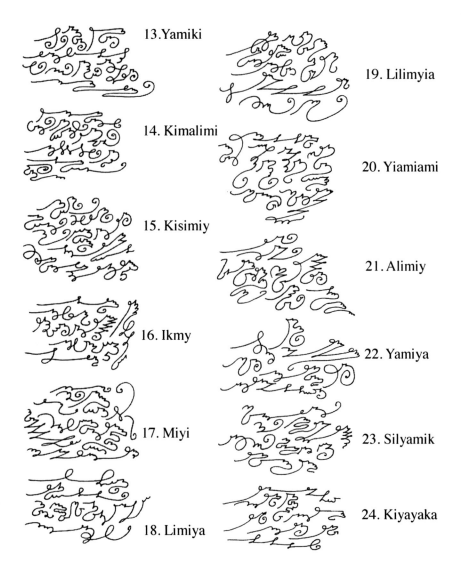

13. Yamiki

14. Kimalimi

15. Kisimiy

16. Ikmy

17. Miyi

18. Limiya

19. Lilimyia

20. Yiamiami

21. Alimiy

22. Yamiya

23. Silyamik

24. Kiyayaka

Guardian Lords of Light (continued)

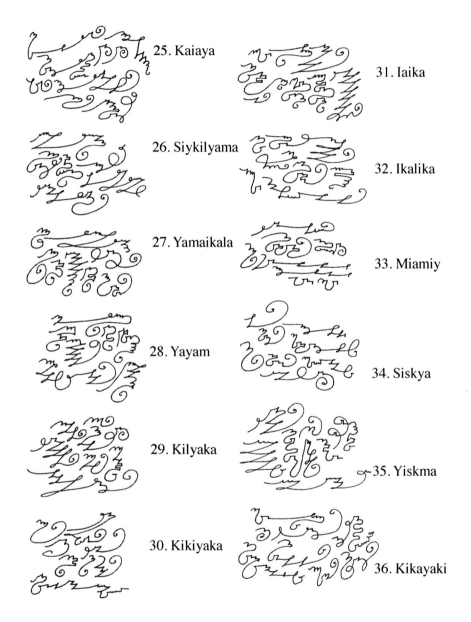

25. Kaiaya

26. Siykilyama

27. Yamaikala

28. Yayam

29. Kilyaka

30. Kikiyaka

31. Iaika

32. Ikalika

33. Miamiy

34. Siskya

35. Yiskma

36. Kikayaki

Guardian Lords of Light (continued)

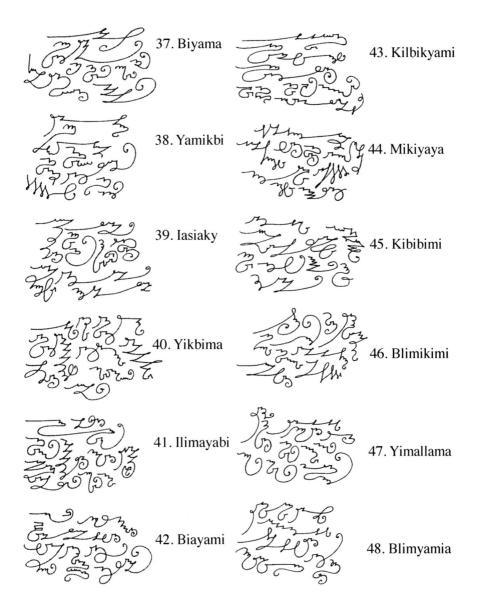

37. Biyama

38. Yamikbi

39. Iasiaky

40. Yikbima

41. Ilimayabi

42. Biayami

43. Kilbikyami

44. Mikiyaya

45. Kibibimi

46. Blimikimi

47. Yimallama

48. Blimyamia

Guardian Lords of Light (continued)

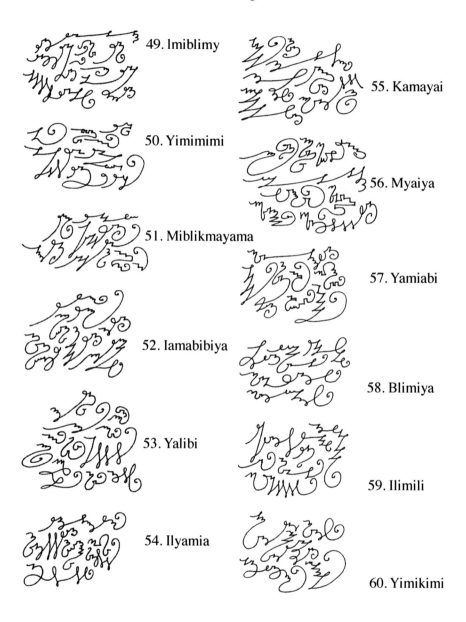

49. Imiblimy

50. Yimimimi

51. Miblikmayama

52. Iamabibiya

53. Yalibi

54. Ilyamia

55. Kamayai

56. Myaiya

57. Yamiabi

58. Blimiya

59. Ilimili

60. Yimikimi

Guardian Lords of Light (continued)

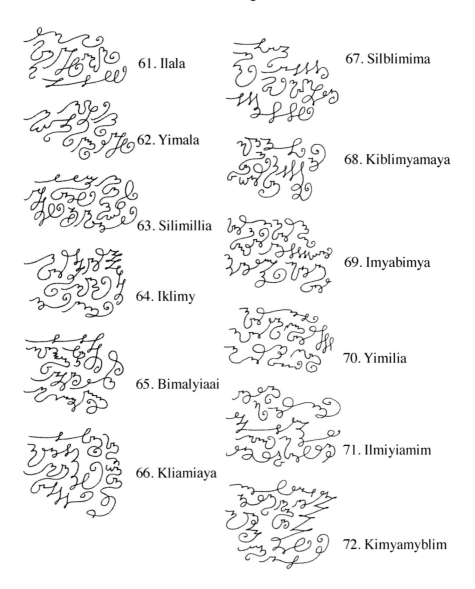

61. Ilala

62. Yimala

63. Silimillia

64. Iklimy

65. Bimalyiaai

66. Kliamiaya

67. Silblimima

68. Kiblimyamaya

69. Imyabimya

70. Yimilia

71. Ilmiyiamim

72. Kimyamyblim

Guardian Lords of Light (continued)

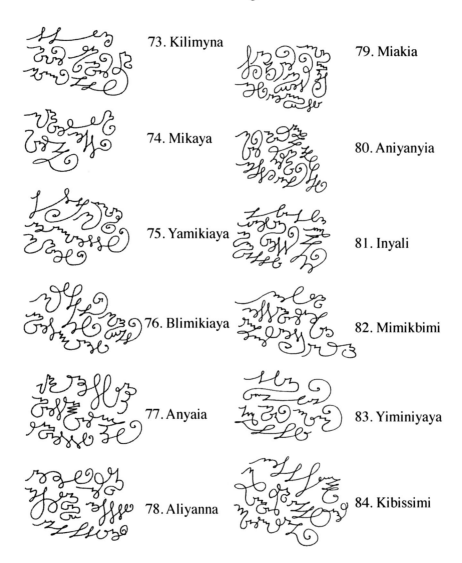

73. Kilimyna

74. Mikaya

75. Yamikiaya

76. Blimikiaya

77. Anyaia

78. Aliyanna

79. Miakia

80. Aniyanyia

81. Inyali

82. Mimikbimi

83. Yiminiyaya

84. Kibissimi

Guardian Lords of Light (continued)

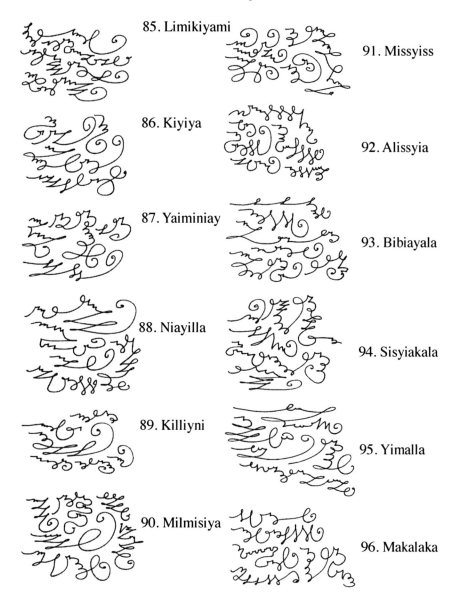

85. Limikiyami

86. Kiyiya

87. Yaiminiay

88. Niayilla

89. Killiyni

90. Milmisiya

91. Missyiss

92. Alissyia

93. Bibiayala

94. Sisyiakala

95. Yimalla

96. Makalaka

Guardian Lords of Light (continued)

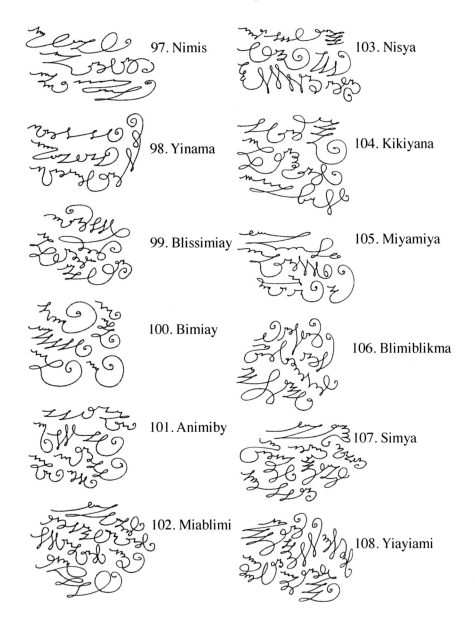

97. Nimis

98. Yinama

99. Blissimiay

100. Bimiay

101. Animiby

102. Miablimi

103. Nisya

104. Kikiyana

105. Miyamiya

106. Blimiblikma

107. Simya

108. Yiayiami

Closing

The greatest asset cultivated with painstaking care by Toltec warriors has always been their impeccability and their fluidity. Both were put to the ultimate test during the culmination of ages of illusion.

It requires the utmost humility and dedication to truth to acknowledge that the dedicated teachings of yesterday, shared with so much conviction by Naguals everywhere, have become obsolete virtually overnight.

Having taught for so long that there is no point of arrival, only to find that in many ways there really is, has illuminated a subtle form of identity: Toltecs shun identity and personal labels, yet many have identified themselves by that which they do. They see themselves as warriors against illusion, and now that illusion has ceased to be, they still cling to the old ways.

Proving myself wrong almost daily has become a way of life. But I know that for change to register that dramatically, life has to be lived at its epicenter; the place where life is always fresh and new, and reality is always in a state of fluid transfiguration. Having weathered the storms of his or her testings, the true Toltec must flower in full potential.

With deep respect to the
Light-bearers of Earth.

"Baalish heresvi uklachva nenuvit"
May absolute truth lead us on.

The Twelve Hidden Planets

BONUS SECTION

The Twelve Hidden Planets[7]

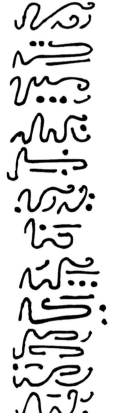

1. Huspave — New Beginnings

2. Kruganet — Inclusiveness

3. Uvelesbi — Alignment

4. Kaanigvit — Empowerment

5. Hubelas — Guided Action

6. Piritnet — Engendered Support

7. Vaa-usta — Universal Cooperation

8. Graanuchva — Manifestation

9. Bru-aret — Triumphant Intent

10. Selbelechvi — Restoration of Magic

11. Husvaa — Discovery

12. Minut — Expansive Vision

7. For more information about the twelve planets, see www.astrology-of-isis.com

The Twelve Feminine Aspects
of the Hidden Planets

1. Ganeesh   Purity

2. Subava   Serenity

3. Minavit   Surrender

4. Pirneef   Release

5. Galbruk   Faith

6. Setbalvi   Hopeful Expectations

7. Nunertu   Patience

8. Giritpa   Gladness of Heart

9. Valveesh   Fluidity

10. Usbatopf   Effortless Accomplishment

11. Elekvru   Delight

12. Sibelvi   Adoration

The Twelve Masculine Aspects
of the Hidden Planets

1. Sfadurchptapr

2. Hmtoupeex

3. Fingtfs

4. Labiyz

5. Tttv

6. Aeyaioauiauieuia

7. Gir

8. Topf

9. Mcbstfre

10. Dopsissv

11. Aiiiqxqwqii

12. Ho-me

Compassion

Reverence

Creativity

Absolute Truth

Impeccability

Celebration

Timing

Focus

Strength

Grace

Clarity

Harmlessness

From the Libraries of Isis: The Wheel of Astrology[8]

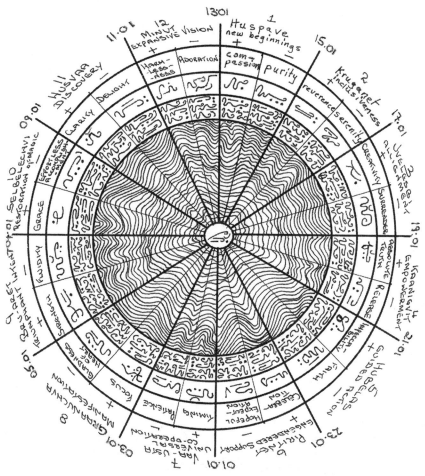

When Planetary Influences are Dominant
(In Your Local Time Zone)

Planet Number 1 Huspave: 13:01-15:01
Planet Number 2 Kruganet: 15:01-17:01
Planet Number 3 Uvelesbi: 17:01-19:01
Planet Number 4 Kaanigvit: 19:01-21:01
Planet Number 5 Hubelas: 21:01-23:01
Planet Number 6 Piritnet: 23:01-01:01

Planet Number 7 Vaa-usta: 01:01-03:01
Planet Number 8 Graanuchva 03:01-05:01
Planet Number 9 Bru-aret 05:01-07:01
Planet Number 10 Selbelechvi 07:01-09:01
Planet Number 11 Husvaa 09:01-11:01
Planet Number 12 Minut 11:01-13:01

8. For more information about the Wheel of Astrology, see www.astrology-of-isis.com

201

The First Planet: Huspave

Dominant from 13.01 to 15.01 hours
Total planetary influences: New Beginnings
Used to influence left ankle
Masculine aspect: Compassion
Feminine aspect: Purity

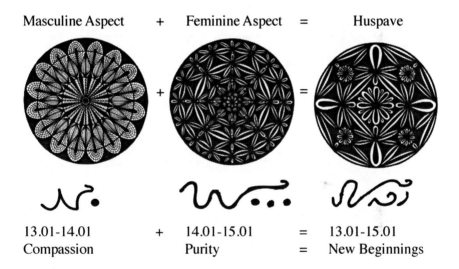

| Masculine Aspect | + | Feminine Aspect | = | Huspave |

| 13.01-14.01 | + | 14.01-15.01 | = | 13.01-15.01 |
| Compassion | | Purity | = | New Beginnings |

Description:
    The planetary surface has red, black and white stone spheres (about 2 inches in diameter). They are very smooth. The black ones are male; the red are female. The white ones are infantile and have not yet chosen a gender. They live in colonies that look like pyramids. There are thousands of these colonies on the surface.

The Second Planet: Kruganet

Dominant from 15.01 to 17.01 hours
Total planetary influences: Inclusiveness
Used to influence right ankle
Masculine aspect: Reverence
Feminine aspect: Serenity

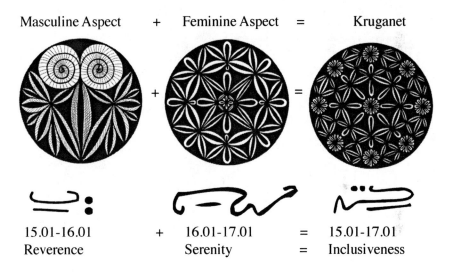

| Masculine Aspect | + | Feminine Aspect | = | Kruganet |

| 15.01-16.01 | + | 16.01-17.01 | = | 15.01-17.01 |
| Reverence | | Serenity | = | Inclusiveness |

Description:
 Kruganet is primarily a water planet, populated by Mer people and also a variety of sea beings like whales, dolphins, fish and others.

The Third Planet: Uvelesbi

Dominant from 17.01 to 19.01 hours
Total planetary influences: Alignment
Used to influence left knee
Masculine aspect: Creativity
Feminine aspect: Surrender

Masculine Aspect	+	Feminine Aspect	=	Uvelesbi
17.01-18.01	+	18.01-19.01	=	17.01-19.01
Creativity		Surrender	=	Alignment

Description:
    The planet looks as though it is completely covered in a fog. Etheric looking, semi-transparent beings populate this planet. They are called Subita. They are about 2-3 feet tall, very light in color. They float slightly above the surface of their planet.

The Fourth Planet: Kaanigvit

Dominant from 19.01 to 21.01 hours
Total planetary influences: Empowerment
Used to influence right knee
Masculine aspect: Absolute Truth
Feminine aspect: Release

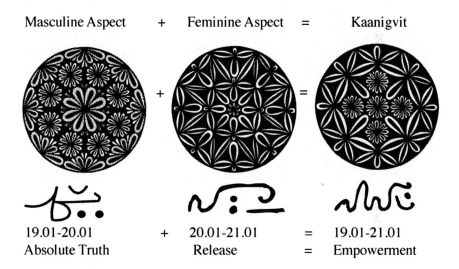

Masculine Aspect	+	Feminine Aspect	=	Kaanigvit
19.01-20.01	+	20.01-21.01	=	19.01-21.01
Absolute Truth		Release	=	Empowerment

Description:

Kaanigvit very closely resembles present Earth with oceans and other bodies of water and landmasses covered with lush vegetation. It is populated by fairies, elves and other small beings.

209

The Fifth Planet: Hubelas

Dominant from 21.01 to 23.01 hours
Total planetary influences: Guided Action
Used to influence left hip
Masculine aspect: Impeccability
Feminine aspect: Faith

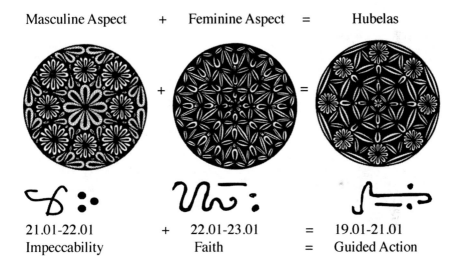

Masculine Aspect	+	Feminine Aspect	=	Hubelas
21.01-22.01	+	22.01-23.01	=	19.01-21.01
Impeccability		Faith	=	Guided Action

Description:
   The planet looks yellow - like the Sahara - being covered with high, yellow sand dunes. It is very hot and there are no life-forms on the surface, but snake-like beings live under the surface.

The Sixth Planet: Piritnet

Dominant from 23.01 to 01.01 hours
Total planetary influences: Engendered Support
Used to influence right hip
Masculine aspect: Celebration
Feminine aspect: Hopeful Expectation

Masculine Aspect	+	Feminine Aspect	=	Piritnet

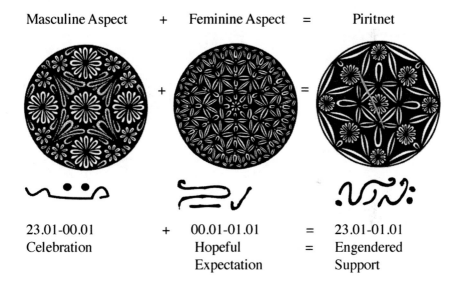

23.01-00.01	+	00.01-01.01	=	23.01-01.01
Celebration		Hopeful Expectation	=	Engendered Support

Description:
   A pinkish planet with a very flat surface. Rainbow colored, luminescent bubble-like beings that look like soap bubbles populate the planet. They are about 3-4 inches in diameter. They emit light, bounce and roll all over the planet.

The Seventh Planet: Vaa-usta

Dominant from 01.01 to 03.01 hours
Total planetary influences: Universal Cooperation
Used to influence left wrist
Masculine aspect: Timing
Feminine aspect: Patience

Masculine Aspect	+	Feminine Aspect	=	Vaa-usta

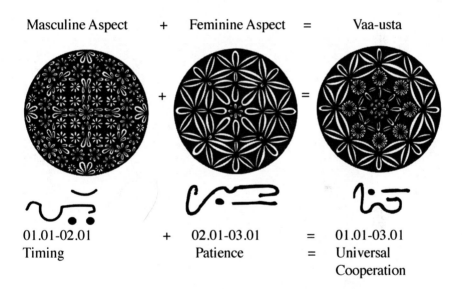

01.01-02.01	+	02.01-03.01	=	01.01-03.01
Timing		Patience		Universal Cooperation

Description:
    The planet is populated by "Furby"-like beings, looking like furry bears. They are between 1-2 feet tall. Pristine forests cover the entire planet, resembling our rain forests. It has butterflies and a large variety of birds in it.

The Eighth Planet: Graanuchva

Dominant from 03.01 to 05.01 hours
Total planetary influences: Manifestation
Used to influence right wrist
Masculine aspect: Focus
Feminine aspect: Gladness of Heart

Masculine Aspect   +   Feminine Aspect   =   Graanuchva

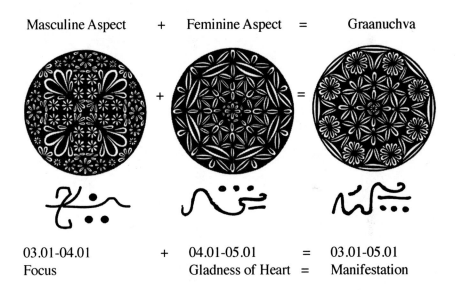

03.01-04.01	+	04.01-05.01	=	03.01-05.01
Focus		Gladness of Heart	=	Manifestation

Description:
   Graanuchva is a very cold planet with water frozen in wave shapes. The ice looks like clear crystal. There are beings called the Taapf that live in underground cities. They are humanoid, about 2 feet tall with roundish bodies and faces.

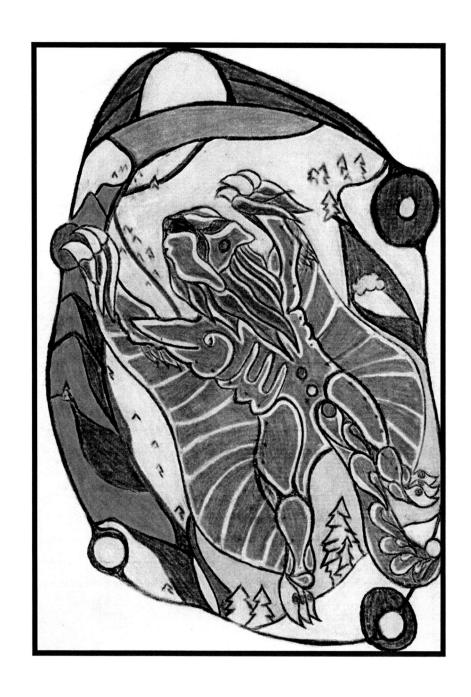

The Ninth Planet: Bru-aret

Dominant from 05.01 to 07.01 hours
Total planetary influences: Triumphant Intent
Used to influence left elbow
Masculine aspect: Strength
Feminine aspect: Fluidity

Masculine Aspect   +   Feminine Aspect   =   Bru-aret

05.01-06.01   +   06.01-07.01   =   05.01-07.01
Strength   Fluidity   =   Triumphant Intent

Description:
    Bru-aret appears has a black, dark grey color. It is populated by tall black humanoid-looking beings. They are 8-9 feet tall with pointy heads. They live in cities with tall buildings that look like skyscrapers. The cities look like square mountains when seen from afar.

The Tenth Planet: Selbelechvi

Dominant from 07.01 to 09.01 hours
Total planetary influences: Restoration of Magic
Used to influence right elbow
Masculine aspect: Grace
Feminine aspect: Effortless Accomplishment

Masculine Aspect	+	Feminine Aspect	=	Selbelechvi

07.01-08.01	+	08.01-09.01	=	07.01-09.01
Grace		Effortless Accomplishment	=	Restoration of Magic

Description:
    The sand is blue and lies in waves as though in the bottom of the ocean. There are very tiny insects (bug-like life-forms) between the grains of sand.

221

Glacier
B.C Dec 3

The Eleventh Planet: Husvaa

Dominant from 09.01 to 11.01 hours
Total planetary influences: Discovery
Used to influence left shoulder
Masculine aspect: Clarity
Feminine aspect: Delight

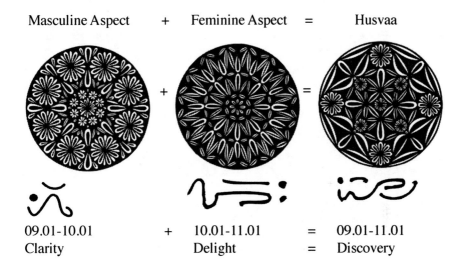

Masculine Aspect	+	Feminine Aspect	=	Husvaa
09.01-10.01	+	10.01-11.01	=	09.01-11.01
Clarity		Delight	=	Discovery

Description:
    This is a green planet with mineral life only. The stones look like malachite. They communicate by sending spark-like electrical light between the rock formations.

The Twelfth Planet: Mi-nut

Dominant from 11.01 to 13.01 hours
Total planetary influences: Expansive Vision
Used to influence right shoulder
Masculine aspect: Harmlessness
Feminine aspect: Adoration

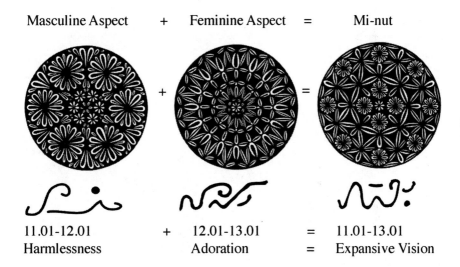

Masculine Aspect	+	Feminine Aspect	=	Mi-nut

11.01-12.01	+	12.01-13.01	=	11.01-13.01
Harmlessness		Adoration	=	Expansive Vision

Description:

This is a planet populated by slim humanoid beings 6-8 feet tall. The planet is brown with a very harsh environment. There are gardens that consist of low bushes with branches without leaves.

The Thirteenth Planet: Klanivik

It pulses during the 2nd hour of every two-hour period
It influences the neck joint
The purpose of its influence is to deepen potential

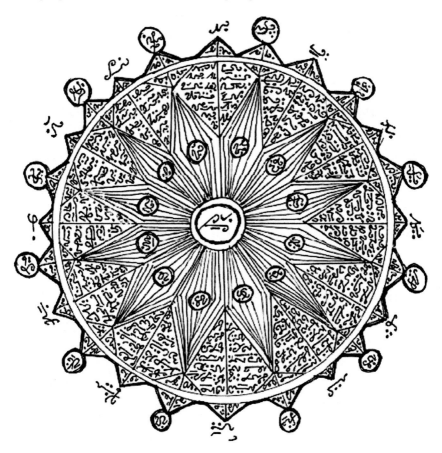

Description:
The Hollow Earth is called by the Hopi 'The Land of the Smoky Sun'. Large populations live in the Hollow Earth[9]. Klanivik is the little sun at the core of the Earth. It pulses every second hour.

9. See *Secrets of the Hidden Realms* for maps

Other books by Almine

Journey to the Heart of God: Mystical Keys to Immortal

Mastery
Published: 2005, ISBN: 978-0-972433-12-9

Secrets Of The Hidden Realms: Mystical Keys to the Unseen

Worlds
Published: 2006, ISBN: 978-0-972433-13-6

The Ring of Truth Second Edition: Sacred Secrets of the Goddess
Published: 2007, ISBN: 978-1-934070-08-6

Arubafirina: The Book of Fairy Magic
Published: 2007, ISBN: 978-1-934070-00-0

The Gift of the Unicorns: Sacred Secrets of Unicorn Magic
Published: 2007, ISBN: 978-1-934070-01-7

Opening the Doors of Heaven: The Revelations of the Mysteries

of Isis
Published: 2008, ISBN: 978-1-934070-13-0

Windows Into Eternity: Revelations of the Mother Goddess
Published: 2008, ISBN: 978-1-934070-23-9

Life of Miracles: Expanded Second Edition
Published: 2008, ISBN: 978-1-934070-96-3

Una Vida de Milagros: Segunda Edición Ampliada (Spanish)
Published: 2008, ISBN: 978-1-934070-14-7

The Thought that Fractured the Infinite: The Genesis of

Individuated Life Published: 2009, ISBN: 978-1-934070-17-8

CDs by Almine

The Power of Silence
The Power of Self-Reliance
Mystical Keys to Ascended Mastery
The Power of Forgiveness

Order books and CDs by phone 502-499-0016 or on our website
www.spiritualjourneys.com

Almine's Websites

Almine Healing
http://www.alminehealing.com

Ancient Shamanism
http://www.ancientshamanism.com

Animal Healing
http://www.spiritual-healing-for-animals.com

Arubafirina
http://www.arubafirina.com

Ascended Mastery
http://www.ascendedmastery.com

Ascension Angels
http://www.ascensionangels.com

Astrology of Isis
http://www.astrology-of-isis.com

Belvaspata
http://www.belvaspata.org

Divine Architect
http://www.divinearchitect.com

Earth Wisdom Chronicles
http://www.earthwisdomchronicles.com

Incorruptible White Magic
http://www.incorruptiblewhitemagic.com

Life of Miracles
http://www.lifeofmiracles.com

Mystical Kingdoms
http://www.mysticalkingdoms.com

School of Arcana
http://www.schoolofarcana.org

Way of the Toltec Nagual
http://www.wayofthetoltecnagual.com

Wheels of the Goddess
http://www.wheelsofthegoddess.com

Printed in the United States
153913LV00004B/6/P

9 781934 070567